77

Emotional Well-Being Micro-practices

Ebrahim Mongratie

Contents

Ground yourself
Send peace into the World
The energy of love, peace, and joy
A strong, sturdy, and healthy body
Worthy of everything good
A problematic situation
Connect to the divine energy of God
Emotional well-being breath-work
Basic breathing
Conscious breathing
Three out-breaths
A sigh of relief
Multiplying love
Baby breathing
Extend the exhale
Pausing the exhale
Alternate nostril breathing
Breathe in the infinite Universe
Higher conscious meditative state
Breathing in love, peace, and joy
Clearing the mind
Full body breathing
Stepping into the future
Optimism
What do you want?
Your ideal future
Visualize it daily

Just like me

Send kindness to your younger self

Loving Kindness

Holding a space for others

Mindful conversation

Inner voice

Taming the voice

Meditation

Counting the exhale

Promoting inner peace

Meditate with the Mudra of life

Moving energy in your body

Relaxing your crown

Body scan

Amplify the love

Use your wings

Power of the Sun

Seven-day program

Day one

Day two

Day three

Day four

Day five

Day six

Day seven

"A grateful heart releases an abundance
of good into your life"

Introduction

My determination to master the art of emotional wellbeing has led me to a few processes that instantly change negative emotion to blissful sensations.

Before this finding, I spent a great deal of my time trying to improve my emotional wellbeing. During this period of my life, I have experienced moments of bliss and inner peace. I say moments as the one thing that stayed constant was my old habits and negative patterns, which seemed almost engraved into my subconscious mind. The negative patterns inevitably brought me back to wanting to find inner peace again.

Each time this happened, I prayed and tried to think positively; this did help a bit; however, my negative patterns quickly kicked in again.

When I found a way that positively changed everything for me, my negative patterns disappeared, and I found a way to experience bliss as my default state. All my emotional trauma cleared.

Through the process of reading this book and trying out the micro-practices, you too can change your default state to bliss and give the world your true fabulous self.

The book is filled with practical processes to enhance your emotional wellbeing. If you are willing to do the work and practice what I teach in this book, your life will positively change.

I designed this book in such a way that it helps you whenever you need guidance, speak to your heart and say, "Guide me to the process that is best for me today." Randomly open the book to any page, find one of the practices on that page, or the one nearest to that page and spend 2 to 3 minutes practicing. Or read what is on that page, and all will make sense to you.

We begin with clearing negative patterns from your past and giving you the ability to change any unwanted behaviours about yourself. We then explore and guide you to envisage a better future for yourself and, finally, how to live mindfully with profound inner peace.

These three components will increase your overall happiness and sense of fulfilment.

You will be able to overcome many complex emotional problems such as depression, anxiety, stress, and even self-loathing. You will then have the tools to deepen the connection with virtually everyone in your life on an intimate, social, and also on a professional level.

This book encompasses a complete learning experience with practical guidelines and a wide range of techniques to get you practicing immediately.

Everything is about to change for you positively. Are you ready?

The journey begins with a 3 step process.

Put yourself in a childlike, playful state.

-

Step into the energy of feeling excellent & successful.

-

Inhale and visualize gratitude

Step one:

While reading this book and practicing the techniques, it is essential to put yourself in a childlike, playful state, which is one of the key ingredients to making a shift in consciousness.

Think about a child. If you know one, picture the child in front of you. Notice how the child is generally always in a playful state. They absorb information like a sponge; the child has a fertile imagination and almost always gets what he or she wants.

A child's sense of independence and self-hood make them primed to challenge rules and go against the norms of society. Be like a child, and the contents of this book will help you make some phenomenal positive changes in your life.

This book is not about getting you to be more childlike. Still, it is the fundamental component of creating emotional wellbeing energy. You will understand this concept as you progress through reading the book.

An adult who does not make time to play is prone to depression and a feeling of being stuck. I suffered from depression, and at that time of my life, I was taking life too seriously, the concept of being playful was ridiculous to me. Looking back at that time, I lacked more than just inner peace; I lacked creative innovation and a sense of humour.

Step two:

Step into the energy of feeling excellent & successful.

Think about the last time you felt amazing. A time when you got that job, promotion, when you succeeded at something, you created a plan, and everything worked out exactly as you planned. Didn't you feel proud of yourself?
Now go back to that feeling and, at the same time, try and stand the way you were standing when you felt so amazing. Remember, a playful state is required.

Now imagine the energy of that feeling in front of you. It is in the form of a square. Reach out and grab hold of it with both hands, make it bigger and lower it to the floor so that you can step into the square. Step into it and lift it to the top of your head and leave it there. The energy field is now permanently there for you to tap into whenever you need it. Next time you feel down, connect to the energy, and you are going to feel amazing again.

Another way to step into good vibrational energy

is to change your body language, and the victory posture is perfect for this.

Hold the following victory pose for 2 minutes.

After 2 minutes, you have no choice but to feel good, try it out and see what I mean.

Step three:

Inhale and visualize gratitude; this is an essential step. Throughout this book, I will be reminding you to practice this fantastic and very beneficial process.

Inhale through your nose while saying **I am grateful** in your mind. Do this three times and then close your eyes and visualize the things you are grateful for, E.g., I am grateful for my bed. Picture your bed and see yourself sleeping on it and being grateful. What else are you grateful for today?

This simple practice has brought me so much inner peace and contentment that I have made it a morning, afternoon, and evening ritual.

These three steps are the basics and a fundamental daily practice that you should adopt if you want to maintain emotional well-being.

Important

Do the following before performing any of the micro-practices. Breathe in, and as you breathe out, focus on the area in front of your nose for 5 seconds.

Stepping outside of yourself

In this section, I will guide you through a few processes of stepping outside of the chaos. Outside of yourself and into a state of awareness of self. A place where you will be able to see things from a new perspective and make decisions without judgment of self and others.

Step into peace
Micro-practice #1

T hink about a situation where you were dealing with a negative person or situation. Think about the situation and try and bring back all the feelings that you experienced in that situation. The scenario you choose is crucial as I want you to experience the beauty of stepping out of the situation on demand.

The next step is to imagine that you are on the top floor of a building. The top floor of the building represents your chaotic situation or person. Now imagine that you are going down to the ground floor of the building. You instantaneously get there and see the person that represents peace for you, someone you trust. This person embodies all your values, and when you are in their company, you are always yourself.

From chaos, you have now stepped into peace. Look up to the top floor of the building and notice how different things are. What do you see? Do you see things from a new perspective?

Take the feeling of the ground floor experience and go back up to the top floor but before you do so, take both hands, reach out and grab hold of the energy around you and place it into your heart. Once again grab hold of the energy around you and put it into your pockets or merge the energy into anything you can keep on you.

To merge energy - Breathe the energy into your heart, hold your breath for four seconds while holding the item in your hands. Exhale the energy into the item and hold your breath for four seconds.

You now have a sense of peace and tranquillity to better deal with the person or situation on the top floor.
Next time you are in a similar situation, know that you can quickly go down to the ground floor to experience some peace to better deal with the situation. You are always in control.

Finding a new perspective
Micro-practice # 2

R ead through this and thoroughly understand the process before you attempt to take yourself through the practice. However, I highly recommend you ask somebody else to guide you through the steps outlined in the process, ask a loved one or a friend to help you out. The person needs to be very patient with you, have a calm voice and a peaceful demeanour.

Find a comfortable space where you will have no distractions. Breathe in through your nose and exhale through your mouth for as long as you can. Please close your eyes and think about a problematic situation that you are currently experiencing or something that you previously experienced but have not made peace with it. Bring up all the feelings that got you down. Immerse yourself back into the situation, when you ready, take note of yourself and imagine that you are now stepping outside of yourself and taking three steps back. You now see yourself in the situation unaffected by the drama. You see things from a whole new perspective. What do you notice? Look around you, do you see anything you may not have noticed before?

When you ready step outside of this version of yourself and take another three steps back. You now see two versions of yourself, and you can now see things from another perspective.

Take note of each version of yourself. Watch what is unfolding in the first situation from the perspective of this version of yourself.

Ask yourself, what can I do differently in the situation, knowing what I know now?

When you ready, and before you step back into the various versions of yourself - Beam love into the version of yourself directly infront of you. To do this - place your right hand on your heart, breathe in and as you breathing in say love in your mind. Hold your breath for four seconds and as you exhale, beam the energy of love from your heart into the version of yourself directly in front of you.

Step forward and merge with this version of yourself.

Beam love into the next version of yourself and merge again until you back into the real version of yourself.

Notice how different you are feeling; you now

have a new perspective on the situation.

Breathe in and exhale for as long as you can.

Becoming your role model
Micro-practice # 3

For this exercise, I remind you about step 1 from the introduction (Step into a child-like, playful state)

For this practice, we are going to play make-believe or role-playing.

Who is your role model? I want you to pretend to be this person for the next minute. If you cannot think of anyone, choose a fictional character like Superman or Wonder Women. By using role models and "pretending to be someone else," you can tap into your dynamic self and begin to change your self-image in a way that you want to see yourself.

Close your eyes and in your mind say "I am now (choose the person you want to be)" Open your eyes and see the world through this person's eyes. How do you think they would be feeling right now? What would they be thinking? Have fun with this and don't take yourself too seriously.

Stepping out of time
Micro-practice #4

Have you ever stepped out of time?
The best way to achieve this is through prayer, meditation, or breathwork. However, the key is to connect your soul to the experience.

Close your eyes and become aware of your body, now become aware that this body has a soul. Note that your soul is energy, and every word you say is energy. Keep your eyes closed and say the word love. Now imagine the energy of love merging with every atom of your body.

Raise your head to the sky, focus on the top of your head and imagine a beam of white light coming down from the heavens connecting you to the entire Universe, see this happening in your mind's eye and feel the energy in your body.
You have now stepped outside of time. Stay in this dynamic portal and make a prayer remembering

that every word leaving your mind or mouth is energy connecting to your soul, your body, and ultimately connecting to the source of all good in the Universe.

Growing into what you want
Micro-practice #5

This process involves stepping outside of your present self and connecting with your future self.

Firstly think about what you want, your goals and if you don't have any goals now is a good time to come up with a least one goal.
Choose a long term goal, perhaps a 5-year goal. Make sure it is a decisive goal, and it is something you want and not something you do not wish to achieve.

With the goal in mind, close your eyes and imagine breathing in time, as you exhale, you enter a time zone two years in the future. In this time zone, you have achieved 50% of your goal.
What does it feel like knowing you have achieved 50% of your goal?

Imagine breathing in time, and as you exhale, you

move into a time zone three years in the future. In this time zone, you have achieved 75% of your goal. What does it feel like knowing you have reached 75% of your target?

Imagine breathing in time, and as you exhale, you move into a time zone one year into the future, in this future time zone, you have achieved 100% of your goal.
Take in the energy of this achievement – well done.

Imagine that you are raising your hands in the air – the victory pose! How does it feel?

You have achieved your goal. In your mind's eye take a look around and notice what is happening, are people congratulating you?

Notice how happy they are for you. Notice how comfortable you are. Everything has turned out entirely perfect.

Clearing negative emotional states

Before I get into these fantastic processes, I remind you about step number 1. (Step into a childlike, playful state) For these practices, it is more important than ever.

Please note that clearing negative energy will not make you permanently happy. In life, happiness comes and goes; when you happy, you eventually become unhappy. Most people only take action when they unhappy, and this is when they finally move forward. However, unresolved emotional states can block people from moving forward. You can quickly and permanently let go of these emotions as they arise.

Before we begin with clearing negative emotions, please spend the next minute, giving positive energy to the world. Stand in front of a mirror and physically send a ball of positive energy to your reflection. Say: "This is for every living being."

Pyramid of emotions
Micro-practice #6

I suggest you get someone to guide you through this practice, taking yourself through it will work as well, but only once you have memorized the process.

Find a comfortable place to sit or lie down. Make sure you have no distractions.
Please close your eyes and imagine you are now in a beautiful forest, it is the most beautiful forest you have ever seen.

As you walk through the forest, you notice a pyramid-shaped building to the left of you. You walk towards it and see a small door in the middle of the building.
As you open the door, a warm and inviting feeling comes over you.
You step inside the pyramid and notice lava flowing down the walls into the ground. On the left of the door, you see a pillar with a red button on it,

labelled, "My experiences."

Reach out and press the button. As you press the button, more pillars raise from the ground all around the room. On top of these pillars are small bottles, some are red, and some are green.

The bottles on each pillar represent your experiences, the red bottles are all your bad experiences, and the green bottles are all your pleasant experiences. Walk towards one of the pillars with the red bottle, pick up the bottle, and notice how soft the glass is, you can reshape the bottle. Reshape the bottle into a ball and throw the ball onto the pyramid wall. As the ball hits the wall, it disintegrates along with the unfortunate experience attached to it. Go ahead and dissolve all the red bottles you see.

Take your time, one by one, hold it in your hand, change the shape to a ball and throw it against the wall.

When all the red bottles are gone, pick up a green bottle. The green bottles represent all your pleasant experiences as you pick up one of the bottles you experience a moment of bliss.

Keep the bottle in your hand, take another one and merge it with the first bottle, as it becomes one bottle the blissful experience gets stronger. Go ahead and join all the green bottles, once they are all merged, hold them close to your heart. Take a moment to enjoy the blissful sensation of all your pleasant experiences.

When you ready, open your eyes and slowly pay attention to the current moment.

Repeat this entire process three times for the next three days and then once a week or whenever you need a moment of bliss.

---

* This micro-practice is based on David Synders grey room.Visit www.nlp-power.com

Put the bad experience behind you
Micro-practice #7

Y ou will need to be standing up while practicing this one; all you need is a place with no distractions and a childlike energy ready to experience something new.

Close your eyes and think about a bad experience. Try to experience all the emotions you felt when the incident or experience took place.

Where in your body do you feel this emotion or pain? Use your index finger and press this area — as you press the location on your body, the pain projects in front of you as a ball of energy.
What colour is the ball of energy?
When you touch the top of the ball, the colour changes to white, and when you rub the bottom of the ball, the colour changes to black. Choose black or white based on which one makes you feel better.

It is now time to take note of the lessons from the bad experience, your subconscious mind has a record of these lessons – when you touch the centre of your forehead, your unconscious mind projects running commentary of the lessons onto the ball. Notice the text scrolling on the ball, and you don't need to read it; however, as you see the text, your conscious mind takes note of the lessons. Spend a few seconds looking at the script, scrolling on the ball, or a few minutes. The projection will stop when you ready to move on.

Take your right hand and slice through the ball of energy as if your hand is a sword. As you do this, the ball breaks into two round balls of energy.

Take the balls with both hands and throw them over your head, behind you. As you throw the balls of energy behind you, they disintegrate along with the emotion. Breathe in and exhale a sigh of relief, do it again and exaggerate the sigh this time.

This practice is fantastic for getting rid of emotions and pain from the past. Next time something from your past comes up, go through this practice.

---

* This micro-practice is based on David Synders magic frame practice. Visit www.nlppower.com

The fact-finding mission
Micro-practice # 8

Many of us have bad habits we accumulated over time. These habits are stored in our subconscious mind and play out in our life over and over. We end up making unconscious decisions, never being aware that we are making these decisions. It is time to clear everything up and make sense of the past.

Imagine you are going on a fact-finding mission back in time. Equipped with Armor that protects you from any negative emotions, equipped with the ability to identify negative beliefs and patterns.

Close your eyes and imagine you are stepping into a fact-finding time machine. The machine is round and covered in black tourmaline crystals. The black tourmaline crystals help with transforming negative energy.

You get into the machine, and it slowly rises. To

the left of the machine is your past, and to the right is your future. For now, the machine is going into your past.

As the journey begins, think about negative patterns in your life. What kind of experiences takes place over and over again? What is the recurring theme in your life? Perhaps its anger towards a particular type of person, or you can't stand certain types of people, and maybe you do not do well with authority figures. Whatever your pattern, think about how it makes you feel; try to remember the last time you felt this way.

As you recall the event, the machine instantly takes you to this event in your past.

You can see this event play out from the machine without being affected by any negativity of the situation. You begin to feel empowered as you watch the circumstances of this incident play out. From this perspective, you can take note of things that you were not able to do before. You take out a note pad and make notes of what you notice.

When you ready, the machine awaits a thought from a time further in your past, a time when you had a similar experience or had the same feeling in your body. As you recall the event, the machine instantly takes you there.

Notice the similarity of this event and witness how things play out. Make some notes of things you may not have noticed before. Write down every detail, make the writing motion in the air and let the pen in your hand flow, don't worry too much of what you write, let the pen do the writing, and you be a witness to the experience. You will know when to stop writing.

It is time to go further back in time, to your earliest memory of this experience, a time when you were just a child.

As you recall this childhood experience, the machine takes you there. You look down from the machine and see a young version of yourself, experiencing the same emotions. Pay attention to what is happening in the event as the younger version of yourself made a decision that changed your future timeline. Focus on this more youthful version of yourself to identify the choice that triggered the pattern. Take a moment to reflect on this, and it will come to you.

Once you have identified the decision the younger you have made, think about something you can tell this younger version of yourself that will change everything, something nobody ever told the younger you. What needs to be said?

Manoeuvre the machine down to the younger you. Step outside, and put your hand on the shoulders of the younger you. Say what you need to say in a way that only you know how to say it.

Now that you said what you needed to go back to

the machine, rise, and look ahead into your future timeline and notice how everything has changed for the better.

The machine takes you back to the future and passes over all the previous incidents that caused you pain, look down, and notice how different things are. Smile and appreciate the change in your timeline.

Automatic meditation
Micro-practice #9

Every person can activate this state by a specific type of breathing – In the next section, we will be focusing on emotional well-being breath-work; however, this particular breathing process fits nicely into this section.

You can access this state by ultimately slowing down the breathing process, it may take time to get the rhythm going, but once you get it – you enter an immediate meditative state. It is beautiful – please practice and don't give up because the automatic meditative state is terrific – your mind completely shuts down.

You will need a timer for this.

Begin by exhaling completely, then:
Breathe in for 20 seconds
Hold your breath for 20 seconds
Exhale for 20 seconds

You will be taking one breath per minute.
If 20 seconds is too long, try 5 seconds and build up from there.

Try one cycle and then 2, build up to 5 minutes of this kind of breathing, and you are going to be acquainted with the Universe, and the Universe is going to become aware of you and your desires.

Reminder

Do the following before performing any of the micro-practices. Breathe in, and as you breathe out, focus on the area in front of your nose for 5 seconds.

Relationships
Micro-practice #10

If you like someone, chances are they have qualities you identify in yourself, or they have similar beliefs as you.

The people that you dislike may have traits you don't like about yourself, or they do things that do not align with your core values, or perhaps they remind you of one of your parents.

Take a moment and identify a person you do not like. What do you not like about them?
You may find that the things you don't like about them are the same things you do or have done before. Please take a moment and think about it, once you identify the habit in yourself or a belief you hold, clean it up. Use micro-practice number 7 for this.

Make the necessary changes to yourself, and the other person will no longer be an issue for you and over time the person may disappear from your life.

Create this new belief –

Say: **I cannot change others but I can change myself.**

Be like a tree
Micro-practice #11

Find a place where you can stand up and hold your hands out to the side.

When you ready, stand up, close your eyes and lift your hands out to the side. Imagine yourself being a tree, say: I am a tree.

You are now a tree, filled with green and brown leaves, the brown leaves represent all the negativity in your life, and the green leaves represent all that is good. Move your arms and let go of all the brown dead leaves, feel them falling, see them falling. As the leaves fall, you feel lighter and at peace.

All that's left is the beautiful green leaves, smile, and enjoy the feeling of being renewed.

Use the energy of the Earth Micro-practice #12

L ay down on the ground, preferably outside on the grass — a yoga mat or towel.

Breathe in, and as you breathe in, imagine the energy of the earth rising into your body. When you exhale, imagine a release of what no longer serves you.

Then say to yourself: "The energy of the Earth revitalizes my body."

Again: Breathe in, and as you breathe in, imagine the energy of the earth rising into your body. When you exhale, imagine a release of what no longer serves you.

Then say to yourself: "The energy of the Earth revitalizes my body."

Repeat this process for 5 to 10 minutes.

Heartful energy
Micro-practice #13

C lose your eyes, breathe into your heart, hold your breath, and focus on your heart.

Try and find your heartbeat; keep your focus on your heart for 20 seconds.

Breathe out slowly. Keep your hand on your heart, and connect to the energy in your heart.

Now imagine that you are filling your entire body with this energy, from head to toe.

Put a smile on your face and send the same power into the world around you.

Tunnel of love
Micro-practice #14

L ove your past, be optimistic about the future, and appreciate the current moment. Close your eyes and say the following words three times:

Love
Optimism
Appreciation

Keep your eyes closed looking to the left of you and say – I send love into my past – as you say it picture hearts or the word love passing through a tunnel – the tunnel represents your past.

Look to the right of you and say: I am optimistic about my future, as you say this picture an energy field of optimism flowing through a tunnel – the tunnel represents your future.

Through a child's eye
Micro-practice #15

C lose your eyes and imagine you are a 2-year- old child.

A happy 2-year-old child, smiling and full of life. What does life look like through the eyes of a 2-year-old child?

Open your eyes and look around you through the eyes of a 2-year-old child. If you see an object, pick it up and look at it with wonder.

Look around you and notice that your eyes see love all around you.
You see a world full of possibilities, your imagination is limitless.

Look at another aspect of your life, home, work or social. What do you see?

Stay in the moment for a while, enjoying the wonder and beauty.

I am abundant
Micro-practice #16

While focusing on your heart say: (*Your first name*) is Abundant – repeat for 30 seconds.

While focusing on your heart, say: (*Your full name and surname*) is abundant – repeat for 30 seconds.

While focusing on your heart, say: I am abundant, I AM. Emphasize the second I AM. – repeat for 30 seconds.

Take a deep breath in through your nose, close your eyes; exhale and say thank you seven times, open your eyes. Say: I am now receiving all the abundance life has to offer. I AM.

Again:
Say: I am now receiving all the abundance life has to offer. I AM.

Again:

Say: I am now receiving all the abundance life has to offer. I AM.

Stream of love
Micro-practice #17

Breathe in and imagine the air going into your heart. When exhaling, imagine a stream of love flowing out of your heart into the rest of the World.

If you don't feel any love right now, try the following:
Place your hand on your heart. Breathe in through your nose, hold your breath for 10 seconds while focusing all your attention on your heartbeat. Do this for 2 minutes.

Keep your hand on your heart, breathe into your heart and in your mind say, love. Breathe out, continue breathing like this for 1 minute.

Touch your throat and say I love myself more and more each day.

Now, imagine the 5-year-old version of yourself standing in front of you.

Take a deep breathe in, as you exhale, imagine a stream of love flowing out of your heart and into the heart of the 5-year-old version of yourself.

Say I love you (your name) - I love you (your name)

You are now ready to send love into the rest of the World: Remember YOU ARE LOVE.

Reminder

*Do the following before performing any
of the micro-practices. Breathe in, and
as you breathe out, focus on the area
in front of your nose for 5 seconds.*

Ground yourself
Micro-practice #18

Connect to the energy of the Earth through grounding.
Do the following bare feet and preferably outside on the grass or sand.

Press your big toes into the ground while breathing in through your nose. At the same time, imagine the rejuvenating energy of the Earth flowing up from your big toes into every cell of your body.

As you exhale, imagine sending the same energy into the world around you, rejuvenating everything your eyes can see.

Do this for a minimum of 5 minutes, be playful, thankful, and joyful.

Send peace into the World
Micro-practice #19

Sit down in a comfortable place, free from distraction.
Breathe in through your nose and exhale through your mouth for as long as you can.

Say the word peace out loud, three times
Say the word peace in your mind three times
Put your hand on your heart and focus all your attention on your heart while saying the word peace in your mind six times.
Keep your hand on your heart and imagine the word peace being written all over your heart. Write the words at your own pace.
Be in the moment and enjoy the experience, make sure that every part of your heart gets the word peace.

You have now created potent energy of peace in your heart. As you breathe out, send this energy into the environment around you and into the rest of the World.

You may want to direct this energy to a specific place or a particular person.

The energy of love, peace, and joy
Micro-practice #20

Begin by stepping into a playful, childlike state, get ready to play make-believe.

Close your eyes and say the word, love, as you say, love, the energy of love comes out of your mouth, you see it in the form of a colourful shape. What colour do you see?

The energy of love is now in front of you. Hold the energy there and move onto the next step.

Say the word peace, and notice the energy of peace coming out of your mouth, in the shape and colour of your choice (first impression)

The power of peace is now in front of you. Hold the energy there, and move onto the next step.

Say the word joy, and notice the energy of joy coming out of your mouth, in the shape and colour of your choice (first impression)

The power of joy is now in front of you. Hold the energy there and move onto the next step.

You now have three shapes in front of you, representing the powerful energy of love, peace, and joy.

Reach out and grab hold of all three energies and merge them into one powerful ball of energy. As you do this, the colour changes, what colour is it? First impression.

Notice what direction the ball is spinning and spin in the same direction 1000 times faster.

Take the ball of energy and move in into your heart.

For a different experience, move the ball of energy all over your body. Shift the energy to the top of your head and down to your feet. Then back up to the top of your head and then into your heart.

A strong, sturdy, and healthy body
Micro-practice #21

Sit down in a comfortable place, free from distraction.
Exhale through your nose three times as quickly as you can.

Close your eyes and focus your attention on your heart. Breathe in and hold your breath. Hold your breath. Listen and feel your heart beating, Once you find your heartbeat, keep holding your breath and say, "My body is strong" over and over again. Do so until you can no longer hold your breath. Breathe in and exhale through your mouth for as long as you can.

Breathe in and hold your breath. Listen, and feel your heart beating. Once you find your heartbeat, keep holding your breath and say, "My body is powerful" over and over again until you can no longer hold your breath. Breathe in and exhale through your mouth for as long as you can.

Breathe in and hold your breath. Listen and feel your heart beating. Once you find your heartbeat, keep holding your breath and say, "My body is healthy" over and over again until you can no longer hold your breath. Breathe in and exhale through your mouth for as long as you can.

And finally.
Breathe in and hold your breath. Listen and feel your heart beating. Once you find your heartbeat, keep holding your breath and say, "My body is strong, powerful, and healthy right now." Say this over and over again until you can no longer hold your breath. Breathe in and exhale through your mouth for as long as you can.

Worthy of everything good
Micro-practice #22

F ind a partner for this practice. You will each take turns to whisper a phrase into each other's right ear.

The phrase is: "You are worthy of everything good in your life." However, before you say the phrase, please mention it to yourself seven times. Say: I am worthy of everything good in my life.

You are saying the words into the person's right ear.

"You are worthy of everything good in your life."

It is essential to say it in the right ear.
The information received by the right ear is processed by the left-hand side of the brain, which is more logical and better at deciphering verbal information.

Take note of how you feel when these words are

spoken to you. Saying these words into the right ear is a positive reinforcement on a whole new level.

A problematic situation
Micro-practice #23

F ind a comfortable place with no distractions. Sit on the floor or on a chair, whichever is more convenient for you.

Breathe in and exhale for as long as you can.
Bring to mind a previous problematic situation or a current one.
Now think about someone who cares about you or think about a public figure you find to be caring.
Imagine this person in front of you, firstly smiling and then responding to your difficulties with warmth and understanding.
Receive their kindness by placing your hand on your heart. Along with understanding, you receive wishes for your well-being and happiness.
Care and concern fill your heart and moves into the rest of your body, enriching every atom of your being.
Say: I love myself – I genuinely love myself; I have

the tools to overcome this situation. I now rise above this situation, and everything works out for my higher good.

Now bring to mind someone you know who is having a difficult time. Smile and send the healing energy of your smile to the person. Allow yourself to feel what you would wish for them. Put your hand on your heart and wish them health, happiness, contentment, or a general wish for their well-being. Imagine them receiving this energy through their heart, enriching every atom of their being with love.

Now expand this energy to anyone in the World experiencing difficulty or pain. Begin by sending them the healing power of your smile. Then say: May their suffering be relieved, and may they be well.
Put your hand on your heart and wish them health, happiness, contentment, or a general wish for their well-being. Imagine the person receiving this energy through their heart, enriching every atom of their being with love.

Breathe in and notice how you are feeling in the body. Notice your head, your neck, your chest, your belly, your legs, and your feet.
End this practice by saying: Thank you.

Connect to the divine energy of God
Micro-practice #24

Find a comfortable place to sit with no distractions.

Close your eyes, put your hand on your heart, and think "infinity."

Focus on your heart and say Love – Love – Love – Love – Love

Now say: God – God – God – God – God - or say the holy name of God you generally use

Keep focusing on your heart and say God – God – God – God – God.

Now, visualize the hand of God, removing the burdens of your heart.

Gives thanks for this incredible blessing, say: Thank you, God – thank you, God – Thank you,

God, thank you, thank you – I love you God – I genuinely love you.

Emotional well-being breath-work

Breath-work is one of my favourite emotional wellbeing enhancers. Breathing in specific ways has allowed me to experience beautiful states of bliss, calmness, clarity, peace, and physical power beyond belief. Before we get into emotional wellbeing breathwork, I want to share the physical power I refer to above, and this is something you can test out right now. You can experience an enhanced physical state or boost of energy on demand by simply breathing in a certain way.

If you have access to a flight of stairs right now, use

it for this experience. Alternatively, try push-ups or planking. Please choose something that will not harm you in any way. When you ready, breathe in the following way throughout the activity.

Breathe in through your nose three times and exhale through your mouth two times, start again: In through your nose three times and out of the mouth two times. Get used to the pattern and then begin your physical activity, breathing like this the entire time. There is no pause in-between each breath, keep the rhythm going

In three and out two and then immediately in three and out two. Your body is now generating more energy.

Some of the upcoming practices involve holding or retaining the breath. Please do not hold or retain your breath if you have been diagnosed with any of the following conditions listed below.

Gastric ulcer, coronary disease, hernia, hypertension, bipolar disorder, recent abdominal or thoracic surgery, anxiety, stroke. Abdominal, pelvic or retinal disease.

Pulmonary disease, epilepsy, pregnancy, lung cancer, lung disease, asthma. chronic bronchitis, aneurysm and dissociative disorder.

Basic breathing
Micro-practice #25

The basics of emotional wellbeing breathwork are to simply learn how to focus on your breath without controlling it in any way. For the next minute, focus on the breathing process. Breathe normally but notice the movement of your breathing. Pay attention to the inhale and the exhalation. Are you breathing in through your nose or your mouth? What thoughts are coming up? As thoughts arise, bring your attention back to the process of breathing. Any sensations in your body? Are you experiencing any feelings?

Put your hand close to your mouth or nose. When you breathe out, notice how the breath feels on your hand.

Think about something that excites you and take note of your breathing. Has it changed in any way? Take a few fast-paced steps, has your breath changed?

Focus on all these changes in your breath.
Think about somebody you love, how are you breathing now?

Play with various scenarios and experiences and notice how your breath changes from one activity to the next.

Conscious breathing
Micro-practice #26

This practice is similar to micro-practice #25; however, for this practice, take full control of your breathing while paying attention to your breath.

Breathe in through your nose and notice how it feels, extend the inhale, and notice how you feel, pause after the inhale and see how you feel.
Notice how it feels when you exhale through your nose very quickly.
How does it feel when you take a long exhale?
How does it feel when you breathe in through your mouth and exhale through your nose.

Take a moment and be playful, be like a child, and play with your breath while paying attention to the feelings in your body.

Three out-breaths
Micro-practice #27

Q uick and easy, three breaths out of the nose as fast as you can. On a scale from 1 to 10, I would say exhale with the force of a 5. Exhale three times, one after the other, and inhale after the three exhales.

Next, try a slower exhale of three breaths. Slow it down, time the exhale so that each exhale is the same length. Try counting as you exhale, 1, 2, 3.

Next, completely slow down the exhale. However, this time exhale through the mouth.
Exhale three times, one after the other, no exhalation until after the 3 three out-breaths. Keep the pause between each exhalation brief as possible.

Now for a few variations:

Mouth – Mouth – nose

Nose – Nose – Mouth

Mouth – nose – mouth

Close the right nostril – nose – nose – mouth

Close the left nostril – nose – nose – mouth

Close the right nostril – mouth – mouth – nose

Close the left nostril – mouth – mouth - nose

Play around with these variations and use the ones you prefer.

A sigh of relief
Micro-practice #28

Give yourself the gift of a sigh – more specifically, a sigh of relief. This process can help you mentally and physically reset your body.

For this practice, remember step #1 (**Step into a childlike, playful state**)

Have fun with the sigh, exaggerate it, smile while doing it, laugh after each sigh. Do it over and over again, sigh like no one is watching you or sigh as your life depends on it.

Try lying down for a different experience. Relax every muscle in your body and take a sigh of relief. Take a few seconds to enjoy the moment, and then sigh again.

Multiplying love
Micro-practice #29

This practice involves some imagination, visualization, and an attitude of sharing.

Close your eyes, and breathe into your heart and hold your breath. Convert the air in your heart into love, multiply the love, make it 100 times stronger.

Then exhale the love through your mouth directing it towards your loved ones and into the World. Smile and imagine every living being receiving your love, including mother Earth.

Again: Close your eyes, and breathe into your heart and hold your breath. Convert the air in your heart into love, multiply the love, make it 1000 times stronger. Then exhale the love through your nose directing it towards your loved ones and into the World.

Baby breathing
Micro-practice #30

If you ever watched a baby sleep, you would have noticed how the baby's belly expands and contracts as they breathe. This type of breathing is the way we are all meant to be breathing, but as we got older, we seemed to have forgotten the natural breathing pattern. Many people unconsciously practice shallow breathing, and this could be due to past traumas that restricted the breathing pattern.

The benefits of going back to baby breathing include improved skin tone, physical longevity, and body detoxification. Furthermore, it builds a deep sense of peace and tranquillity. I suggest easing into this way of breathing, touch the lower part of your stomach, focus on that spot while breathing in for 3-5 seconds, and out for 3-5 seconds. Set a timer and breathe like this for 5 to 10 minutes.

Make this a daily practice and slowly increase the in-breath to 20 seconds and out-breath to 20 seconds. The body can make a positive and profound life-altering shift when you extend your breath to 1 minute in and 1 minute out.

Extend the exhale
Micro-practice #31

When I breathe out longer than I inhale, I experience an incredible calming sensation. This form of breathwork is one of my favourites. There are so many forms of long exhales, and I enjoy each one. The first and most obvious is the simple process of exhaling through the mouth for as long as possible. Work up to a minute of exhaling to experience a fantastic state of inner peace.

Next, try exhaling as if you are blowing out of a straw or thin pipe, it generates a beautiful feeling. Try exhaling an aaaaahhhhhh sound, slowly and as long as possible.

Then the Ohhhhhhh sound, in the same way, and then the Mmmmmmm sound, slowly and as long as possible.
As you exhale these sounds, make sure you create

a vibration in your body, this enhances the entire process.

Practice extending your breath by counting in your mind as you exhale. Begin with counting to 10 and stretch it over time.

If you want to live a healthier, well-balanced life, take longer breaths.

Pausing the exhale
Micro-practice #32

Holding on to the exhale is powerful.
I enjoy the feeling I get when holding my breath after the exhale.
It feels so much better than holding the breath after the inhale.

Try it out for a few seconds and then lengthen the pause for as long as possible.

Set yourself a high target and work towards that.

This method is known to heal asthma and help with panic attacks and anxiety.

* Please do not hold or retain your breath if you have been diagnosed with any of the following conditions listed below.

Gastric ulcer, coronary disease, hernia, hypertension, bipolar disorder, recent abdominal or thoracic surgery, anxiety,

stroke. Abdominal, pelvic or retinal disease.
Pulmonary disease, epilepsy, pregnancy, lung cancer, lung disease, asthma. chronic bronchitis, aneurysm and dissociative disorder.

Alternate nostril breathing
Micro-practice #33

Alternate nostril breathing is an ancient breathing technique that has a therapeutic effect on your health. You can feel the positive effects of it almost immediately.

Begin by blocking your left nostril with your right ring finger, exhale through your right nostril and then inhale through your right nostril. Immediately block your right nostril with your right thumb and exhale through the left nostril and inhale through the left nostril.

Immediately block your left nostril with your right ring finger, exhale through your right nostril and then inhale through your right nostril. Block your right nostril with your right thumb and exhale through the left nostril and inhale through the left nostril.

Continue switching between the two nostrils for 10 minutes.

To have a completely different experience with alternate nostril breathing, try the following.
Block your left nostril with your right ring finger, breathe in and out rapidly for about 3 seconds. Block your right nostril with your right thumb and breathe in and out quickly for about 3 seconds. This type of breathing generates a fantastic feeling.

Breathe in the infinite Universe
Micro-practice #34

For this practice, you are going to breathe in the entire Universe and exhale everything that is within you, back into the Universe.

This is a beautiful experience, enjoy every second of it.

Close your eyes, think about, and picture the entire Universe. As you breathe in, imagine breathing in the whole Universe, into your heart.

Breathe out, and as you breathe out, imagine breathing out the entire Universe back into its place.

Again: Close your eyes, think about, and picture the entire Universe. As you breathe in, imagine breathing in the whole Universe, into your heart.

Breathe out, and as you breathe out, imagine breathing out the entire Universe back into its place.

Higher conscious meditative state Micro-practice #35

Before you begin with this micro-practice, learn the rhythm of this process.

Lie down and breathe the following way for 2 minutes. Once you complete the practice, please close your eyes, and allow the feeling in your body to transport you to a beautiful place, go with it and enjoy it.

Breathe in through your nose and exhale through your nose.

Breathe in through your nose and exhale through your mouth.

Breathe in through your mouth and exhale through your nose.

Breathe in through your mouth and exhale through your mouth.

Two minutes of this micro-practice, close your

eyes and enjoy the feeling.

Breathing in love, peace, and joy
Micro-practice # 36

Close your eyes, picture love in front of you, the image of what love represents for you, bring on the feeling of love if you can. What colour is it? Is it moving? What direction is it spinning? When you notice the direction, turn it faster, 100 times more quickly. When you ready, breathe it into every cell of your body, picture it circulating inside of you. Open your eyes.

Picture **peace** in front of you. Close your eyes, the image you see represents peace for you. Bring on the feeling of peace if you can. What colour is it? Is it moving? What direction is it spinning? When you notice the direction, turn it faster, 100 times more quickly. When you ready, breathe it into every cell of your body, picture it circulating inside of you. Open your eyes.

Picture **joy** in front of you. Close your eyes, the image you see represents joy for you. Bring on the feeling of joy if you can.

What colour is it?
Is it moving?

What direction is it spinning? When you notice the direction, turn it faster, 100 times more quickly.

When you ready, breathe it into every cell of your body, picture it circulating inside of you. Open your eyes.

Clearing the mind
Micro-practice # 37

Find a comfortable place to sit with no distractions.

Close off your right nostril with your right thumb and inhale deeply through your left nose. Exhale completely through your mouth.

Then, inhale very slowly and exhale even more slowly. Continue for 30 seconds and exhale through the nose three times as quickly as you can. All the while keeping your thumb closing off the right nostril.

Keeping your right nostril closed with your right thumb, inhale deeply through your left nose. Exhale completely through your mouth.

Continue this process for 6 minutes.

Full body breathing
Micro-practice #38

Find a comfortable place with no distractions. Sit on the floor or on a chair, whichever is more convenient for you.
Close your eyes and take a full breath in and a long breath out. Please focus on the breath and allow it to move your body as you inhale and exhale. Don't take control of your breathing; allow the process to flow with the divine nature of your being.

Now, as you breathe in, imagine that your whole body is breathing in. As you breathe out, believe that the entire body is breathing out. Imagine every atom of your being breathing in and every atom of your being breathing out. Continue this process for a minute. After a minute, hold the breath and notice the sensations that are alive in your body.
On the next exhalation, gently open your eyes and slowly move your hands and then your legs.

Gently lift your head up and then down.

Then say the word LOVE a few times.

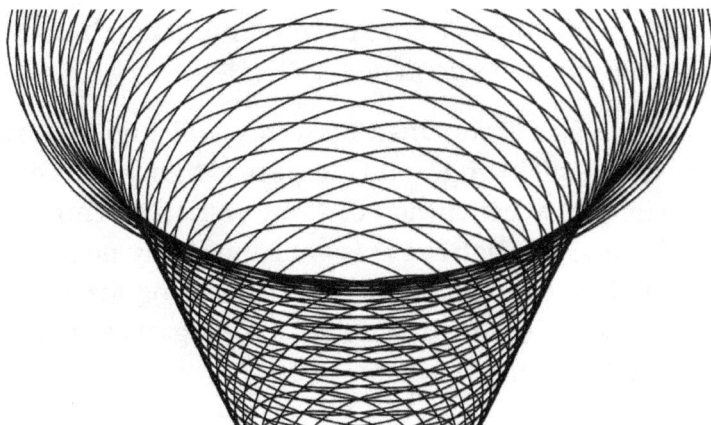

Stepping into the future

I often wondered if I truly have the power of free will. Is my future in my own hands? Or in my ability to envisage a certain future. Or is my life destined to play out in a certain way?

After much reflection on free will, and learning about various cultures and religions, I believe that I do have the power of free will. I also think that my future does lie in my own hands. Destiny plays a part as well; however, prayer can change destiny. I believe that thinking about and envisaging a best possible future is a sort of prayer and can help to impact our lives positively.

There was a time when I had no goals, no vision, no desires. Throughout that period of my life, I experienced everything I did not want and things I did not like. I believe this was due to my negative thoughts. Unconsciously I was praying for negative energy via my thoughts, and negative energy is what I received.

However, when I consciously changed my thoughts and envisioned a fantastic future, I noticed a considerable change in my life.
I found that the act of stepping into the best possible future was an incredibly important part of my emotional wellbeing.

Optimism
Micro-practice # 39

The foundational practice of the best possible future is optimism. Be optimistic about the future.

Thoughts of optimism and the feeling of being optimistic is an essential part of this practice.

Close your eyes, and begin with the thought of being optimistic about the future.

You can say the words, "I am optimistic about the future, I AM," Your conscious mind might reject this, but keep on saying it. "I am optimistic about the future, I AM."

Again: "I am optimistic about the future, I AM."

Without hesitation, bring on a feeling of optimism, and imagine everyone on the planet being optimistic, see everyone with a smile on their faces. Imagine and feel the combined planetary power of positive energy flowing through you and to all those seeking the same energy.

Spend a few minutes in this state and enjoy the energy of optimism flowing through your body.

Be grateful for this energy, and send gratitude to the Universe.

What do you want?
Micro-practice #40

To be able to live your best possible future, you must know what you want. If you don't see what you want, you will get more of what you don't want.

This practice is about identifying what you want and then writing it down.

Spend some time reflecting on what you want and make sure you eliminate thoughts of what you do not want. Choose one goal that seems impossible or something that makes you feel uncomfortable.

This step is essential for the next practice, and I encourage you to spend a lot of time on this. Review what you want daily and add on to your list daily. Most people spend more time thinking about what they do not want in their lives, and they end up getting more of what they do not want.

Your ideal future
Micro-practice # 41

Now that you know what you want, it is time to step into your best possible future. As you breathe in, say the following in your mind, "Five years from now." Hold your breath, close your eyes, and imagine yourself being transported to a timeline five years from today. As you arrive in the future, breathe out and merge with your future self. You notice everything you set out to achieve is playing out exactly as you planned. Notice who you have become.

Look around.
Who is around you?

How do you feel? Spend some time identifying what your relationship with others has become. Open your eyes and write down everything you noticed, you will need this for the next practice.

Visualize it daily
Micro-practice # 42

A fantastic future begins with a vision of how your life will look and how you are going to feel when you get there. It is like a dress rehearsal but in your mind's eye.

From today you will need to sit down in a quiet place and transport yourself to your best possible future and see it play out in your mind as if you are watching a movie. Use what you wrote down in the previous practice and play the movie in your mind.

This time add feelings to the experience. What will it feel like living your best possible future?

Stand up and align your body language to your best possible future self. Perhaps you are standing up straight with your shoulders back and looking up. Maybe you are pumping your fist in the air, and raising your hands in a victory pose. Act like your best possible future self.

Remember to make this a daily practice until your reality merges with your best possible future.

Regular practice is the key to building this future, to better understand this, think about a tomato seed or any seed of your choice. One day you decide to plant the seeds in your garden. What do you think your expectations of the seed will be? Are you going to expect to get a tomato tree the next day or the next week? No right? You understand the process of growing a tree, and it doesn't happen overnight. You will need to water the seeds daily, make sure it gets enough sunshine, and nurture the soil. It takes around six to eight weeks to grow tomatoes from seed.

The same goes for your ideal future, understand that nature takes time with your ideal future as well. You will need to focus on your ideal future daily. Making sure it plays out in your mind daily and making sure you experience the feeling of the outcome in your body daily. What's more, this process will make your day to day issues more comfortable to get through and increase your happiness and wellbeing.

If your life is challenging right now, you should create an affirmation of your ideal future.

When I was going through a difficult time, I envisioned a better future and visualized it once a day. However, it was not enough because my predominant thoughts were about my issues at the time. Thankfully I recognized this and created an affirmation that reminded me about my ideal future. Every time I thought about my problems, I repeated my affirmations, which made a massive difference in my life.

If you can't come up with an affirmation, use the following one. "My life is now merging with my ideal future" When you say this picture a moment from your ideal future. Doing this is an excellent distraction from your negative thoughts.

Action
Micro-practice # 43

If you want to swim, you will have to dive into the pool.

Depending on your goal, choose a date to take action, and when that date comes, take action. I did this for the first public workshop I ran. I set a date and ran with it even though I had no experience with public speaking. Fifty people turned up, and I did the best I could at that moment in time. After the workshop, I said to myself, "Well done, Ebrahim, that was amazing. You did well."
I messed up here and there, but I chose not to focus on the negative. Instead, I gave myself positive feedback, and later in the day, I reflected on what I could have done differently.

Had I chose not to step into the unknown and run the first workshop, I would probably still be contemplating doing it. I messed up a few times, but I am glad I decided to start the process of putting myself out there.

Living a Mindful Life

Becoming a self-guided being

A while ago, I was driving down the road, and suddenly somebody cut in front of me, immediately a deep sense of fear gushed through my body. I immediately took evasive action by hitting the brakes and steered away. As the emotion of fear faded, I got to the point of decision:

Do I get angry?

Do I get revenge?

Do I show my anger to the other driver ? Or Become aware that I just had a huge fright, take a deep breath, and allow myself to merge into the energy of calmness.

To my later disappointment, I chose option one. I got angry even though in my mind, I told myself option 4 is better for everyone. The feeling of anger was a choice I made, and when I made this choice, my emotion of anger amplified. I focused on anger, but I did not want this emotion. I mean, nobody wants to be angry. I blamed the other driver for my feelings, and this prevented me from identifying and improving the cause of the emotional effect.

A while later, I realized that focusing on the feeling was my downfall here.

One of my core values is **Respect**, and it is this value that ultimately produced a bad feeling about the anger I experienced.

The lesson I took from this experience is that focusing on my core values instead of the feeling would have made me feel a lot better.

I decided to make focusing and appreciating my values a habit. When I trust my values, I feel authentic and empowered, and this seems to bring me an abundance of joy.

My core values are:

Trust
Honesty
Courage
Fairness
Respect
Caring

When I violate these values, I experience feelings of guilt, shame, and anxiety.

Core values
Micro-practice #44

The first step here is to choose a few core values that you live by, write them down. Mine are Trust, Honesty, Courage, Fairness, Respect, Caring.

You can choose a daily practice or weekly practice. Using the values, I listed above or your own, close your eyes, and breathe in through your nose as you breathe in, say the word trust. As you exhale, say the word trust in your mind and then ponder on what trust means to you and how you can you live the value of trust, e.g., I keep my promises; therefore, I am trustworthy.
Follow this process with all the values you have written down.

Focusing on your values is one of the best ways to

feel good on a day to daily basis.

Conscious questions
Micro-practice # 45

Part of mindful living is to occasionally think about yourself on your death bed and ask yourself some conscious questions.

Close your eyes and picture yourself on your deathbed. It may take a while for you to get into this space, but please try as this process can help you make significant positive changes to your life.

As you lie there, knowing you are about to die, ask yourself:
Does my family know how much I love them? and when last did I look them in the eye and say the words, "I love you."

Am I proud of how I lived?
Did I enjoy the experience of being human?
Did I forgive him/her/them?
Did I pray enough for others?
Was I faithful to my core values?

The one thing I am most grateful for is.

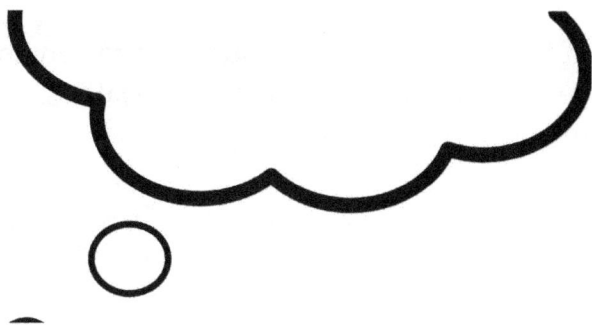

Conscious Thoughts

J ust like the breath, thoughts arise without any
effort or conscious intention. You can momentarily take control of your breathing, and
I believe you can take control of your thoughts
too.

Thoughts generally arise from our memories, beliefs, knowledge, attitudes, and reasoning. Then
you have those thoughts that are false and run
counter to beliefs and logic, the voice in your head
can quickly become the enemy within. When this
happens, you do not have to beat yourself up for
having these thoughts.

It is in your power to start to take control and release what is unwanted and unhealthy.

Affirmations
Micro-practice # 46

Affirmations are the best form of conscious thinking. I love repeating affirmations for emotional well-being.

Affirmations quickly sink into the subconscious mind and create new situations and circumstances. It seems so basic and straightforward, but it is incredibly powerful and has uplifted me many, many times.

Say the following affirmation 100 times:
Everything is well and good in my life.

The beauty of this affirmation is that after a while of saying it, a feeling gets generated that makes you feel good, but you have to say it at least 100 times.

I strongly suggest saying it 300 times a day if you are struggling emotionally.

I am good at
Micro-practice # 47

Find a comfortable place to sit with no distractions.

Breathe in through your nose and exhale through your nose. Continue breathing like this while focusing on your breath. At the same time think about what you are good at (Your strengths)

Say: I am
Say: I am
Say: I am
Say: **I am good at** (?) Say as many things that come to mind.
All the while, focusing on your breathing.

This practice is essential and incredibly uplifting. If you are struggling to find things you are good at, please take a moment to reflect on it and write it on a piece of paper. Once you have everything written down, begin the practice.

Mindful eating
Micro-practice #48

E ating healthy is essential; however, mindful eating is much more critical.
Before I explain mindful eating, please ponder on the following scenario.

It is Monday, at 6 pm, you get home from a hectic day at work. Thankfully dinner is sorted, and you sit down in front of the television to have a meal with your wife, husband, or partner. You say grace or bless the food in the name of God and begin to eat. As you eating a conversation starts about your day, in great detail, you talk about your bad experience and relive the day. Unknown to you, the negative energy of your day mixed with the drama of your favorite soapie playing on the TV merges with your food. You finish your meal in less than 3 minutes and don't end up sleeping well that night.

This scenario may seem reasonable to many people. However, it is far from it and extremely dangerous.

Everything is energy, and when you combine negative energy with your food, the negative energy becomes apart of you.

Be peaceful when you eat, and you will become more peaceful. Do not watch TV or consume digital content while eating. If you really must, make sure you are watching or consuming digital content of a positive nature.

Try relaxing while eating and use all your senses throughout the experience.

Examine your food by touching it with your hands or using cutlery.

Look at your food and enjoy the colors.

If you are eating hot food, listen to the food sizzling.

Chew the food slowly and keep each bite in your mouth for a few extra seconds, enjoying the flavors, and finally enjoy the smell of your food.

Mindfully eating will enhance your emotional well-being.

Peace
Micro-practice # 49

F ind a comfortable place to sit with no distractions.

Connect the tip of your thumb to the tip of your ring finger, use both hands. Rest your arms on your lap. Think about peace and say the following words:

I am peace
I radiate peace
I love peace

Keep the thought of peace in your mind and say the following phrases over and over for 2 minutes.

I am in peace. **I AM** x3
I radiate peace. **I DO** x3
I love peace. **I DO** x3
Peace is all around me. **IT IS** x3
Peace is within me. **IT IS** x 3
I bless myself with peace. **I DO** x 3

I bless others with peace. **I DO** x 3
Every atom of my being dances to the rhythm of
peace. **THEY DO** x3

Prosperity thoughts
Micro-practice #50

Having thoughts of prosperity can create a prosperous world around you. It begins with the belief that you are prosperous. Say the following out loud "I am prosperous, I live a flourishing life of success and good fortune surrounds me" Emphasize the words, *Prosperous*, *Flourishing*, *Success*, and *Fortune*.

For the next 5 minutes, keep the above words in your thoughts.

Sit on the floor or in a comfortable chair, with your back straight. Set a 5-minute timer.
Join the tip of your ring finger with the tip of your thumb, do this on both hands.
Say the following "I am prosperous, I live a flourishing life of success, and good fortune surrounds me."

Then say the words one by one: ***Prosperous, Flourishing, Success, Fortune.***

Say these words over and over or think only about these words and the statement above. Allow no other thought into your mind. If your mind wanders, bring it back to the words.

When the 5 minutes are over:

Breathe in through your nose and in your mind say "Prosperous" (*do not exhale yet*)

Breathe in through your nose and in your mind say "Flourishing" (*do not exhale yet*)

Breathe in through your nose and in your mind say "Success" (*do not exhale yet*)

Breathe in through your nose and in your mind, say "Fortune," then exhale.

Repetition is essential. I encourage you to practice this in 5-minute intervals for no more than 30 minutes at a time.

When you think prosperity thoughts:

You will begin to see life in a whole new light.

You will discover your inner power

Your health will improve

Your relationships will improve

You will find true abundance in your life.

Your self-confidence will increase.

Thinking these prosperity thoughts every day will trigger a feeling of joy, bliss, and happiness.

Abundance
Micro-practice #51

T hink abundance and know that everything you need will come into your life at its appointed time.

SAY: I can do what I need to do when I need to do it. I have so much to share and so much to spare. I consistently experience abundant love, abundant peace, and abundant joy. I am unconditionally abundant; abundance flows to me whenever I need it. Abundance surrounds me. I am an abundant being. I am grateful for my abundance, thank you, thank you, thank you.

Join your ring finger and your thumb on both hands. Focus all your attention on your heart, and say the following words in your mind.

Abundant Love
Abundant Peace
Abundant Joy
Abundant Wealth

Abundant Happiness

Repeat this for as long as you need to trust your instincts, and you will know when it is time to stop.

Stop looking and start seeing
Micro-practice #52

For this practice, you will need to be in the dark. If you are afraid of the dark, you may keep a small light on but nothing too bright. You will need the room dark enough, but not so dark that you cannot see anything.

Once the room is dark, relax your eyes, don't strain the eyes. Feel for movement and use your sense of hearing. Focus your attention on your sense of hearing. So much so that all you think about is your sense of hearing. Listen for sounds far away and then in the room.
Slowly move around and keep all your attention on your sense of hearing, listening for sounds furthest away, and then in your immediate surroundings. Alternate between the sounds furthest away from you and the ones closest to you.

Using your sense of hearing like this is an excellent practice to quiet the mind.

Relationships

Relationships have been one of the most complex challenges I have ever experienced in life. Over the years, conflict in several relationships has cost me my tranquillity and inner peace. These relationships lacked a strong foundation of unconditional acceptance and trust.

When I grew up, there were no academic lessons on good relationships; instead, I learned everything about relationships from friends and family. Some individuals were not the most excellent role models.

These days good and healthy relationships have become so much more valuable, meaningful, and fulfilling to me. I make sure my connections have a foundation of unconditional acceptance and trust. I accept people for who they are. What's more, is I can respect where the person is in his or her life journey.

Let them know
Micro-practice #53

Think about somebody in your life and say the following words as if you are talking directly to them.

Bring someone to mind, and say:

You are not me, and I am not you.

You get to be you in this relationship, and I get to be me.

I have my interests in life, and you have yours.

You are the expert on your life, and I am the expert on mine.

I respect where you currently are in your life; please show me the same respect.

Every atom in my body dances to the rhythm of peace. THEY DO x3

Nobody but me
Micro-practice #54

Find a comfortable place to sit with no distractions.

Put your hand on your heart and say the following, speaking directly to your heart.

Nobody can control my choices but for me. Nobody can maintain my honour but me. Nobody can manage my truth but me.

Nobody can maintain my self-control or responsibility but me. Nobody can execute my vision and faith, but for me.

Say: I am – I am – I am

Again: Nobody can control my choices but for me. Nobody can maintain my honour but me. Nobody can manage my truth but me.

Say: I am – I am – I am

Active listening
Micro-practice #55

Which one of your relationships requires some TLC? Practice the following with this person. It is a practice of active listening.

You will each get 3 minutes to talk while the other person listens attentively, making eye contact the entire time. The listener is not allowed to say anything except when the person has nothing else to say; in this instance, the listener should say, "What Else?" This question allows the other person an opportunity to think.

Decide on a topic to discuss – Perhaps ask one of the questions below and set a 3-minute timer.

I motivate myself by

I'm not too fond of it when

I love it when...

I honour others by...

Let me tell you what's in my heart

I have the following on my mind

You can practice this with someone you love as well, and it works wonders for married couples.

Blessings
Micro-practice #56

S end blessings of love, peace, and joy to somebody you love. Think of the person and say, "I bless you with love, peace, and joy." Think about somebody you don't like and say, "I bless you with love, peace, and joy." Repeat it, and this time touch your heart while saying it. "I bless you with love, peace, and joy."

Whomever, you see today, look at them and say, "I bless you with love, peace, and joy."

Perhaps you at a coffee shop, look around, choose someone and say, "I bless you with love, peace, and joy."

If you at an airport or in a mall, choose some-one and say, "I bless you with love, peace, and joy." Then send the same blessings to everybody around you.

Finally, say it to yourself, "I bless myself with love, peace, and joy."

Mindful breathing
Micro-practice #57

When I began practicing mindfulness meditation, I noticed a considerable improvement in all my relationships. I soon appreciated how my thoughts and actions impact relationships. Try it for yourself.

Find a quiet place where you won't be disturbed. Sit in a chair with your back straight and feet flat on the floor; close your eyes, and observe your breath. Notice how it feels when you breathe in through your nose and exhale through your nose. When your mind wanders off, bring your attention back to your breath.

It's normal for your mind to wander off; be mindful of when it does happen and bring it back to the process of observing your breath.

Begin with 5 minutes per day and gradually increase to 15 minutes per day. It helps if you practice this at the same time every day.

Before you respond
Micro-practice #58

Next time someone says something that upsets you, take three breaths before you respond.

Make sure it is three complete breaths, inhale and exhale. The longer you prolong the exhale, the more power you gain to choose your response.

You can enhance the power of response by focusing on a central point while breathing. I suggest you focus on the area just in front of your nose. The breathing and focused attention will momentarily disconnect you from your internal world and external world.

Practice this often to stay disconnected longer.

Gratitude

Whenl consciously enter a state of gratitude, I experience pure bliss and serenity, which positively impacts my overall experience of happiness and well-being.

I noticed that negative energy is unable to prosper when I settle into a grateful state.

What's more, is that gratitude considerably elevates my self-esteem and optimism. For this reason, I make gratitude a daily practice, and I am grateful for everything, including things like the Moon, the stars, the butterflies, and the bees.

Gratitude
Micro-practice #59

The best time for this practice is in the morning and the evening before bedtime. In the morning, begin this practice by saying, "My day begins with gratitude and joy," and if you are doing this practice in the evening, say, "My day ends with gratitude and joy."

You will need to step into a childlike, playful state for this practice and have a glass of water nearby, not a full glass, just enough for a few sips.

Sit up in your bed, close your eyes, and imagine stepping into a blue space ship. As you step into the spaceship, you see a pink spacesuit, purple space boots, and an orange Helmut. You put these on, and as you sit down in the yellow seat, you are automatically strapped in with a red seatbelt. The shuttle takes off and flies to the Moon.

The flight to the Moon takes a few seconds, and

the space ship lands safely on the Moon. Full of excitement, you get out and walk towards finding a panoramic view of the Earth. The spectacular view takes your breath away. You stand there frozen in time, eyes wide open, amazed by the beauty of the Earth.

Your heart opens like never before.

All you think about is how grateful you are.

Say thank you three times and begin this gratitude practice.

Thank you for the beautiful Earth; it is spectacular.

Thank you for this moment – I love this moment, thank you.

Thank you for the divine blessing that allows me to be here.

Thank you for this beautiful planet. I get to call home. The atmosphere, the picturesque sky, the clouds, the rain, the thunderstorms, the snow, the rainbows, the sunsets, and the sunrises, thank you.

Thank you for the resources on Earth. Thank you.

Thank you for Summer, Spring, Fall (autumn) and winter

Thank you for the Oceans and all the beautiful creatures dwelling therein, not forgetting the beach sand, the waves, the ships, boats, submarines, and the lighthouses, thank you.

Thank you for the feeling of freedom and safety I enjoy every day.

Thank you for gravity on Earth, keeping me grounded and holding the Mountains in place. I love the Mountains. Thank you.

Thank you for the forests, Jungles, National parks, botanical gardens, valleys, and the countryside.

Thank you for Budapest, Cairo, Cape Town, Hallstatt, Rome, Lisbon, San Francisco, Santiago, Tokyo, and all beautiful cities in the world, including small towns and townships. Thank you.

Thank you for the flowers, those that blossom in purple and blue, thank you for the trees and those that shed leaves of orange, red and brown.

Thank you for the oxygen that keeps me alive.

Thank you for all living creatures on Earth, I especially love the Dolphins and Blue Whales, the butterflies and birds, the polar bear cubs and Koala bears. Cats, dogs, and those cute Penguins thank you.

Thank you for the deserts, dunes, coves, and caves.

Thank you for the tall breath-taking buildings, the Pyramids, magnificent walls and monuments, thank you.

Thank you for electricity and oil and the automobiles that get me around.

Thank you for the planes, helicopters, hot air balloons, and jets.

Thank you for books, articles, blogs, newspapers, magazines.

Thank you for the food I consume daily, the water I drink. Special thanks to the fruit I love, and the vegetables and spices, Ice cream and chocolate, thank you. Take a few sips of the water.

Thank you for the sound of laughter, the sound of kids having fun, and their beautiful smiles.

Thank you for music, art, and stories that uplift me, thank you.

Thank you for all my teachers, the lessons, the growth, the failures, and the accomplishments, thank you.

Thank you for my family, friends, and loved ones. A special thank you to my parents.
Thank you for my heart, my grateful heart. I love this grateful feeling in my heart, thank you, thank you, thank you.

And, thank you for this beautiful Moon.

Once again, give thanks for the divine blessing that allows you to experience this moment on the Moon. With a feeling of bliss, you walk back to the space ship and fly back to Earth. Drink the last bit of water in your glass.

Thank you.

Practice this daily.

Journaling

A few years ago, I started journaling for 2 minutes a day.

On the third day of journaling, I experienced a positive shift in emotional wellbeing, and I often smiled involuntarily.

The process helped me to prioritize my problems, fears, and concerns.

I began by writing whatever came to my mind and then about my day. Eventually, I chose various topics to write.

Each one of these processes allowed me to step

into a fantastic blissful state.

Free flow journaling
Micro-practice #60

Get yourself a journal, empty book, or something to write in.

Hold the book in front of you and say, I bless this book with love, peace, and joy.
Then say – I am now divinely guided and protected.

Set a 2-minute timer and write down whatever comes to your mind, anything and everything after 2 minutes spend some time reflecting on what you have written.

Do this every day and gradually increase the time spent on the journaling practice.

Structured journaling
Micro-practice #61

The previous practice was free-flow journaling, and this practice is structured journaling. Write about any of the following topics:

Before you begin, step into a playful, childlike state, smile, and start writing.

The things I love are

The things that annoy me

My current challenges are

I feel uniquely alive when

When I am at my best I

My favourite way to spend the day is

The things that make me smile are

I cannot imagine my life without this

Writing from a different perspective
Micro-practice #62

This practice involves writing a letter to yourself from the perspective of a close friend. Choose someone who knows you well, someone that understands you and wants the best for you.

Write about the challenges and opportunities you are facing?

Begin by becoming the person. You are now an actor or actress playing the part of this person, close your eyes and say I now see things from the perspective of (their name). As you open your eyes, you see the world through their eyes and begin to write the letter.

When you have done, close your eyes and say thank you (the person's name) for this valuable information. Then open your eyes and reflect on what you have written.

Kindness

The conscious practice of being kind will give you a fantastic feeling on demand while allowing you to live in harmony and balance with all living creatures in the world. What's more, you will be creating an environment of confidence, and everybody will benefit, including yourself.

Kindness will make your soul happy and ease your heart. Every atom of your being will receive healing energy from the universe, as well as feel-good chemicals from your body. The chemicals and healing energy flow through your body for the duration of the act or state of kindness.

Kindness gets easier with practice, and when it becomes a habit, you get even more feel-good chemicals.

The energy of kindness
Micro-practice #63

Say: I radiate the energy of kindness and contribute to an environment of confidence.
Say this as much as possible today and notice how people react to you.

Again: I radiate the energy of kindness and contribute to an environment of confidence.

Again: I radiate the energy of kindness and contribute to an environment of confidence.

Again: I radiate the energy of kindness and contribute to an environment of confidence.

Every time you exhale, imagine sending kindness into the world. Your energy of kindness will continue to spread and uplift all living beings, long after you stop focusing on being kind.

Just like me
Micro-practice #64

Close your eyes, breathe in through your nose for 4 seconds, breathe out for 4 seconds, and hold your breath for 4 seconds. Do a few more rounds of this breathing until you feel calm and settled. Think of a person outside of your social circle or family.

With this person in mind say:

Just like me… "person's name" is a person who has rights.

Just like me… "person's name" has his/her thoughts and ideas.

Just like me… "person's name" wants to be happy.

Just like me… "person's name" wants to live in freedom.

Just like me… "person's name" wants to be safe.

Just like me... "person's name" wants to be free from pain and suffering.

Just like me..."person's name" has a right to privacy.

Just like me..."person's name" wishes to be loved and love freely.

Just like me, "person's name" longs for connection and friendship.

Just like me..."person's name" has at some point in his/her life felt pain, been stressed, and has been ill.

Just like me..."person's name" wants to be kind and caring.

This practice can elevate your mood and allow you to experience kindness, connection, and positivity.

Send kindness to your younger self
Micro-practice #65

Find a comfortable place to sit with no distractions.Place your right hand on your heart and breathe in through your nose for 4 seconds, breathe out of your nose for 4 seconds, and hold your breath for 4 seconds while focusing on your heart.

Imagine and think about yourself as a young child standing in front of you. Close your eyes and say the following to the younger version of yourself.

"May you be blessed with loving-kindness" Breathe in love, and as you breathe out, send the love to your younger self.

Open your eyes and bask in this energy for a while.

Loving Kindness
Micro-practice # 66

Put your hand on your heart and say the following phrases out loud.

May I be blessed with loving-kindness

May I feel whole, complete, and calm

May I accept myself just as I am

May all be well in my World

May the joy of being alive nourish my soul.

May I be abundantly happy.

Now say these phrases in your mind.

May I be blessed with loving-kindness

May I feel whole, complete, and calm

May I accept myself just as I am

May all be well in my World

May the joy of being alive nourish my soul.

May I be abundantly happy.

Next bring to mind someone you love, while reading the phrases, keep your hands in the Lotus mudra position, see image below.
Mudras are symbolic hand and finger gestures that assist the flow of energy in the body while enhancing the meditative journey within.

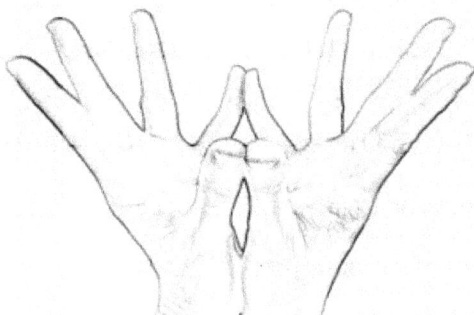

May you be blessed with loving-kindness

May you feel whole, complete, and calm

May you accept yourself just as you are

May you feel the energy of my love now

May the joy of being alive nourish your soul.

May you be abundantly happy.

Now bring to mind somebody you don't know well but see every day, it could be one of your neighbours, a grocery clerk or someone at work. Keep your hands in the lotus mudra position.

May you be blessed with loving-kindness

May you feel whole, complete, and calm

May you accept yourself just as you are

May you feel the energy of my love now

May the joy of being alive nourish your soul.

May you be abundantly happy.
Next, bring to mind someone you don't like. Just for this moment, see if you can let go of feelings of resentment. Keep your hands in the lotus mudra position and say these phrases.

May you be blessed with loving-kindness

May you feel whole, complete, and calm

May you accept yourself just as you are

May you feel the energy of my love now

May the joy of being alive nourish your soul.

May you be abundantly happy.

Next, bring to mind all living beings in the universe. Expand kindness in all directions. Keep your hands in the lotus mudra position and say these phrases.

May all beings be blessed with loving-kindness.

May all beings feel, whole, complete and calm
May all beings accept themselves just as they are

May all beings feel the energy of my love now.

May the joy of being alive nourish every living being.

May all beings be abundantly happy.

Close your eyes, and stay in the energy of kindness for a while. Keep your hands in the lotus mudra position and breathe in through your nose for 4 seconds, breathe out of your nose for 4 seconds and hold your breath for 4 seconds, repeat for a few cycles.

End the session by moving your head side to side, rub your palms together, and finally clench and unclench your fists a few times.

Holding a space for others

I sat there holding my breath, clenching my fist, waiting for her to take a breath so I could get a word in, everything she said made no sense. She didn't stop speaking or wouldn't stop talking, For a moment I stopped listening, and all I saw was her mouth moving and her hands swaying in the air.

It was then when I realized that this moment was not about me; all she needed was someone to hold a space for her.

I suppose she speaks fast and too much because people don't give her a chance to speak; they likely interrupt her like I was about to do.

I took a deep breath, sat back in my chair, and decided not to interrupt her and listen.

She noticed this and sat back and started speaking slightly slower.

I found this interesting, and I was beginning to feel better. I no longer clenched my fist, I surrendered to the current moment, and a feeling of relaxation kicked in.

The incident above happened to me a while ago, and I've had many of these kinds of encounters. As I learn more about being present, I intend to listen more and hold a space for whoever needs it.

Reminder

Do the following before performing any of the micro-practices. Breathe in, and as you breathe out, focus on the area in front of your nose for 5 seconds.

Mindful conversation
Micro-practice #67

C hoose someone you know and ask them to join you for a quick conversation. Tell the person to speak first and tell them to talk about whatever is on their mind.

Imagine creating a white circle around you and the person. It is a circle of trust, safety, honesty, and authenticity. Nothing else can enter this sacred circle.

Focus on the person and your breath. Doing so will keep you in the present moment away from the need to respond.

Now say the following in your mind: "It is not about me, I am non-judgemental" remember to say this to yourself occasionally. Remember to be non-judgemental even if the person seems to be irrational.

Send loving energy to the person, breathe in love, and exhale love towards them.

You may respond only if the person asks you a question. However, if you want this person to like you, repeat some of what they are saying back to them. An example of this is if the person says – "He said the meeting is next week," repeat the same words. "He said the meeting is next week" However, Be careful not to repeat every sentence.

Inner voice

I use to suffer from depression, and during those dark days, I honestly thought my inner voice had different personalities. I called my inner voice, "that guy." I had the what if worrier personality and that guy use to point out everything that can go wrong, he imagined disasters and always expected the worse. Then there was the inner voice that was constantly calling me an idiot, always pointing out my flaws and reminding me of my past failures. That guy was always judging and evaluating my behaviour and comparing me to others. If being called an idiot wasn't enough, that guy kept on telling me I was hopeless, unworthy, and not smart enough. He seemed to love the words, "You can't."

At times that guy was a perfectionist, always pushing me to do better while telling me that my best is not good enough. That guy wanted me to seek acceptance from others, and he did not like me to take action as he expected me to fail.

Thankfully I have learned to control that guy.

Taming the voice
Micro-Practice #68

When your inner voice wants to take over, try not taking it seriously, laugh, and say, "that's not true" when you say this, your inner voice quickly stops feeding you thoughts that are not true. An example of this, your inner voice says something like, "That person does not like me," Use these words, "That's not true."

Practice becoming aware of your inner voice, and when it runs off on a tangent of thoughts, laugh and use the following affirmation:

I only say good things about myself. Say this over and over, and after a while, your inner voice will only say good things about you.

It will take about 21 days of using this affirmation for it to work effectively.

Meditation

I meditate as an act of love for myself and every living being. I connect to Universal energy, submitting to the divine source of pure love and infinite intelligence.

My heart is instantly calmed, filled with serenity, calmness, and love. Time slows down, and I transcend my consciousness into tranquillity and peace. I unwind feeling uplifted, happy, ecstatic, and exalted. All my mental attachments fade away.

Meditation has become one of my daily routines, and I can't imagine a day going by without meditating.

If you want to start a daily meditation practice, begin with the intention. Say: I will meditate daily for the rest of my life. Then start meditating, don't expect to be a perfect meditator right away. It's like learning to play the piano; when you practice, daily, you eventually become an excellent pianist. However, with meditation, you get immediate benefits which include:

Relaxation
Emotional control
Less agitation
A drop in blood pressure
Increase in the sense of wellbeing
An increase in the spirit of connectedness and empathy
It also improves focus and cardiovascular health.

These are just some of the benefits. Once you made the intention to meditate, begin by scheduling your meditations in a planner, calendar, or your phone. Decide on how long you are going to meditate, start small from 2 minutes per session, and gradually increase the amount of time you meditate.
Decide on a morning or evening routine or perhaps both morning and evening. You may also want to add in a mid-afternoon meditation, which is fantastic and helps enhance your emotional state for the rest of the day.

Attach your meditation practice to an existing

habit or routine. Decide on where you are going to meditate formally, I say formally, because you can also informally meditate anytime and anywhere. Informal meditation is merely focusing on your breathing while walking or waiting in line at a grocery store.

Choose a meditation from one of the meditation processes below, try them all and choose your favourite to practice every day.

Counting the exhale
Micro-practice #69

Find a comfortable place with no distractions. Sit on the floor or on a chair, whichever is more convenient for you.

Breathe in through your nose, and then exhale through your nose. Focus on the process of breathing, and the feeling in your body. Thoughts may come and go but always bring your mind back to the manner of breathing.

After 2 minutes of this, start counting the exhale, as you exhale say 1 in your mind, on the next exhale say 2 in your mind, then on the next exhale say 3 in your mind, then 4 and 5. Don't count to 6 but go back to 1, this helps you focus better, and if you find yourself counting past 5, you have wandered off, and that's okay, start from 1 again.

The duration of this practice is entirely up to you.

However, I suggest a minimum of 3 minutes.

Promoting inner peace
Micro-practice #70

Thisʼ practice involves using the yoni mudra. As I mentioned, mudras are symbolic hand and finger gestures, that assist the flow of energy in the body while enhancing the meditative journey within.

Find a comfortable place with no distractions. See picture below, hold this mudra while sitting on the floor or on a chair, whichever is more convenient for you.

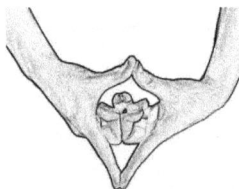

Focus on the voice in your head. Where is the voice? Is it on the left, the right, the center, in front of your head, or behind your head? Wherever the voice, move it to the opposite direction.

You will now have a clear mind and be able to entirely focus on your breathing and the sensations in your body.
Stay in this state for 5 minutes. After 5 minutes, breathe out of your nose three times.

End the session by moving your head side to side, rub your palms together, and finally clench and unclench your fists a few times.

Meditate with the Mudra of life
Micro-practice #71

This practice involves using the mudra of life to assist the flow of energy in the body while enhancing the meditative journey within.

Find a comfortable place with no distractions. Sit on the floor or on a chair, whichever is more convenient for you.
Connect the tip of your ring finger and tip of your baby finger to the tip of your thumb. Place both your hands on your lap, palms facing upwards.

Breathe in and out of your nose, slowly, and focus on the feeling in your body.
In a few seconds, energy will begin to flow, and you will feel the power of the mudra in your hands, moving up your arms. As you breathe in,

move the energy up into your heart. Hold your breath for a moment allowing your heart to multiply the power by 100, and as you breathe out, move the energy from your heart into the rest of your body.

The duration of this practice is entirely up to you. However, I suggest a minimum of 4 minutes.

End the session by moving your head side to side, rub your palms together, and finally clench and unclench your fists a few times.

Moving energy in your body
Micro-practice #72

This practice involves using a mudra to assist the flow of energy in the body while enhancing the meditative journey within.

Find a comfortable place with no distractions. Sit on the floor or on a chair, whichever is more convenient for you.

On both hands close all fingers over the thumb in a fist, hands on your lap palms facing downwards. Connect to your breath and the feeling in your body. You should start feeling the energy flowing.

As you breathe in, move the energy from your hands to the top of your head. As you exhale, move the energy to the soles of your feet.

The duration of this practice is entirely up to you. However, I suggest a minimum of 4 minutes.

End the session by moving your head side to side,

rub your palms together, and finally clench and unclench your fists a few times.

Relaxing your crown
Micro-practice #73

F ind a comfortable place with no distractions. Sit on the floor or on a chair, whichever is more convenient for you.

Place your hands on your lap, palms facing down. Please close your eyes and, in your mind, say: Crown *(which is the top of your head)* I now command you to relax.

We hold a lot of tension in our crown and resting it for a while brings a fantastic sense of relaxation. Feel your crown relaxing. As your crown relaxes, so does your entire body.
Relax into this state and when you ready, breathe in and imagine the air flowing into your crown. When you exhale, blow the air out very slowly as if you are blowing through a straw.The duration of this practice is entirely up to you. However, I suggest a minimum of 4 minutes.

Body scan
Micro-practice #74

This practice involves using the mudra of life to assist the flow of energy in the body while enhancing the meditative journey within.

Find a comfortable place with no distractions. Sit on the floor or on a chair, whichever is more convenient for you. Ask someone to guide you through this or memorize the process first.

Connect the tip of your ring finger and tip of your baby finger to the tip on your thumb. Place both your hands on your lap, palms facing downwards.

Focus your attention on the soles of your feet for 5 seconds.

Focus your attention on the left foot for 5 seconds.

Focus your attention on the right foot for 5 seconds.

Focus your attention on both your legs for 5 seconds.

Focus your attention on your left leg for 5 seconds.

Focus your attention on your right leg for 5 seconds.

Focus your attention on your hips for 5 seconds.

Focus your attention on your lower stomach for 5 seconds.

Focus your attention on your upper stomach for 5 seconds.

Focus your attention on your solar plexus for 5 seconds.

Focus your attention on your heart for 5 seconds.

Focus your attention on your left arm for 5 seconds.

Focus your attention on your right arm for 5 seconds.

Focus your attention on both arms for 5 seconds.

Focus your attention on your neck for 5 seconds.

Focus your attention on your face for 5 seconds.

Focus your attention on your forehead for 5 seconds.

Focus your attention on your ears for 5 seconds.

Focus your attention on the top of your head for 10 seconds. You will begin to feel an energy field or a tingling sensation over your head, move this energy to the ceiling and keep it there for 15 to 20 seconds.
Bring the energy back to the top of your head.

Focus your attention on the right-hand side of your head for 30 seconds.
After 30 seconds, take your thumb and close off your right nostril and breathe normally for 30 seconds while focusing your attention on the right-hand side of your head.

Move your attention to the left-hand side of your head for 30 seconds.
After 30 seconds, take your index finger and close off your left nostril and breathe normally for 30 seconds while focusing your attention on the left-hand side of your head.

End the session by moving your head side to side, rub your palms together, and finally clench and unclench your fists a few times.

The 30 seconds is a guideline, and you can modify this time as you please.

Amplify the love
Micro-practice #75

This practice involves using a mudra to assist the flow of energy in the body while enhancing the meditative journey within.

Find a comfortable place with no distractions. Sit on the floor or on a chair, whichever is more convenient for you.

On both hands clasp a fist and then connect the tips on your thumb and index finger
Place your hands on your lap, palms facing upward.
Imagine breathing love into your heart, hold your breath, and multiply the love by 1000, breathe out the amplified love into the rest of the world.

The duration of this practice is entirely up to you; however, I suggest a minimum of 4 minutes.
End the session by moving your head side to side, rub your palms together, and finally clench and

unclench your fists a few times.

Use your wings
Micro-practice #76

F ind a comfortable place with no distractions. Sit on the floor or on a chair, whichever is more convenient for you.

Step into a childlike, playful state; it is time to play make-believe. Ready?

You were born with wings but have never used them, and for this meditation, you are going to use your wings.
Close your eyes, and bring your wings to the mind. They are attached to your back.

What colour are they?
How big are they?
How fast do they move?

Feel the power of your wings rush through the rest of your body.
Feel yourself rise as you begin to fly, you hover in your current environment. Stay in this moment

for a while and enjoy the feeling.

The rest of this process plays out as you choose. What can you do with these wings? Where can you go? Go there now. Spend the next few minutes going wherever you want to go and do whatever you want to do. When you ready, open your eyes and enjoy the moment.

Now that you know about this energy use it to achieve your goals and come back to this meditation whenever you want to reconnect to this feeling.

Power of the Sun
Micro Practice #77

F ind a comfortable place with no distractions. Sit on the floor or on a chair, whichever is more convenient for you.

Please close your eyes and think about the celes-
tial fireball in our solar system, the Sun. Picture
it in your mind's eye and connect to the energy
of the Sun. As you breathe in, imagine the energy
of the Sun entering every atom of your being. The
power of the Sun consumes everything that no
longer serves you. Breathe in, and imagine the energy of the Sun revitalizing you. Move the energy
around your body and open your eyes when you
ready.

Place your left hand at the bottom of your spine.
Then place your right hand at the top of your
neck.
Connect the energy of the Sun to the base of your
spine and move it with your mind. From the bot-

tom of your spine, slowly up to the top of your spine and back down your spine. Continue this movement for a few minutes. When you have done, exhale very slowly and as long as you can.

End the session by moving your head up and down, rub your palms together and finally clench and unclench your fists a few times.

Seven-day program

Now that you have been through all the micro-practices, I recommend you continue the exercises for the next seven days using the following micro-practices.

Put yourself in a childlike, playful state.

Step into the energy of feeling excellent & successful.

Inhale and visualize gratitude

Important

*Do the following before performing any
of the micro-practices. Breathe in, and
as you breathe out, focus on the area
in front of your nose for 5 seconds.*

Day one

Pyramid of emotions

I suggest you get someone to guide you through this practice, taking yourself through it will work as well, but only once you have memorized the process.

Find a comfortable place to sit or lie down. Make sure you have no distractions.
Please close your eyes and imagine you are now in a beautiful forest, it is the most beautiful forest you have ever seen.

As you walk through the forest, you notice a pyramid-shaped building to the left of you. You walk towards it and see a small door in the middle of the building.
As you open the door, a warm and inviting feeling comes over you.
You step inside the pyramid and notice lava flowing down the walls into the ground. On the left of the door, you see a pillar with a red button on it, labelled, "My experiences."

Reach out and press the button. As you press the button, more pillars raise from the ground all around the room. On top of these pillars are small bottles, some are red, and some are green.

The bottles on each pillar represent your experiences, the red bottles are all your bad experiences, and the green bottles are all your pleasant experiences. Walk towards one of the pillars with the red bottle, pick up the bottle, and notice how soft the glass is, you can reshape the bottle. Reshape the bottle into a ball and throw the ball onto the pyramid wall. As the ball hits the wall, it disintegrates along with the unfortunate experience attached to it. Go ahead and dissolve all the red bottles you see.

Take your time, one by one, hold it in your hand, change the shape to a ball and throw it against the wall.

When all the red bottles are gone, pick up a green bottle. The green bottles represent all your pleasant experiences as you pick up one of the bottles you experience a moment of bliss.

Keep the bottle in your hand, take another one and merge it with the first bottle, as it becomes one bottle the blissful experience gets stronger. Go ahead and join all the green bottles, once they are all merged, hold them close to your heart. Take a moment to enjoy the blissful sensation of all your pleasant experiences.

When you ready, open your eyes and slowly pay attention to the current moment.

Repeat this entire process three times for the next three days and then once a week or whenever you need a moment of bliss.

Day two
Gratitude

The best time for this practice is in the morning and the evening before bedtime. In the morning, begin this practice by saying, "My day begins with gratitude and joy," and if you are doing this practice in the evening, say, "My day ends with gratitude and joy."

You will need to step into a childlike, playful state for this practice and have a glass of water nearby, not a full glass, just enough for a few sips.

Sit up in your bed, close your eyes, and imagine stepping into a blue space ship. As you step into the spaceship, you see a pink spacesuit, purple space boots, and an orange Helmut. You put these on, and as you sit down in the yellow seat, you are automatically strapped in with a red seatbelt. The shuttle takes off and flies to the Moon.

The flight to the Moon takes a few seconds, and the space ship lands safely on the Moon. Full of

excitement, you get out and walk towards finding a panoramic view of the Earth. The spectacular view takes your breath away. You stand there frozen in time, eyes wide open, amazed by the beauty of the Earth.
Your heart opens like never before.
All you think about is how grateful you are.
Say thank you three times and begin this gratitude practice.

Thank you for the beautiful Earth; it is spectacular.

Thank you for this moment – I love this moment, thank you.

Thank you for the divine blessing that allows me to be here.

Thank you for this beautiful planet. I get to call home. The atmosphere, the picturesque sky, the clouds, the rain, the thunderstorms, the snow, the rainbows, the sunsets, and the sunrises, thank you.

Thank you for the resources on Earth. Thank you.

Thank you for Summer, Spring, Fall (autumn) and winter

Thank you for the Oceans and all the beautiful creatures dwelling therein, not forgetting the beach sand, the waves, the ships, boats, submarines, and the lighthouses, thank you.

Thank you for the feeling of freedom and safety I enjoy every day.

Thank you for gravity on Earth, keeping me grounded and holding the Mountains in place. I love the Mountains. Thank you.

Thank you for the forests, Jungles, National parks, botanical gardens, valleys, and the countryside.

Thank you for Budapest, Cairo, Cape Town, Hallstatt, Rome, Lisbon, San Francisco, Santiago, Tokyo, and all beautiful cities in the world, including small towns and townships. Thank you.

Thank you for the flowers, those that blossom in purple and blue, thank you for the trees and those that shed leaves of orange, red and brown.

Thank you for the oxygen that keeps me alive.

Thank you for all living creatures on Earth, I especially love the Dolphins and Blue Whales, the butterflies and birds, the polar bear cubs and Koala bears. Cats, dogs, and those cute Penguins thank you.

Thank you for the deserts, dunes, coves, and caves.

Thank you for the tall breath-taking buildings, the Pyramids, magnificent walls and monuments, thank you.

Thank you for electricity and oil and the automobiles that get me around.

Thank you for the planes, helicopters, hot air balloons, and jets.

Thank you for books, articles, blogs, newspapers, magazines.

Thank you for the food I consume daily, the water I drink. Special thanks to the fruit I love, and the vegetables and spices, Ice cream and chocolate, thank you. Take a few sips of the water.

Thank you for the sound of laughter, the sound of kids having fun, and their beautiful smiles.

Thank you for music, art, and stories that uplift me, thank you.

Thank you for all my teachers, the lessons, the growth, the failures, and the accomplishments, thank you.

Thank you for my family, friends, and loved ones. A special thank you to my parents.
Thank you for my heart, my grateful heart. I love this grateful feeling in my heart, thank you, thank you, thank you.

And, thank you for this beautiful Moon.

Once again, give thanks for the divine blessing that allows you to experience this moment on the Moon. With a feeling of bliss, you walk back to the space ship and fly back to Earth. Drink the last bit of water in your glass.

Thank you.

Day three
Visualize it

A fantastic future begins with a vision of how your life will look and how you are going to feel when you get there. It is like a dress rehearsal but in your mind's eye.

From today you will need to sit down in a quiet place and transport yourself to your best possible future and see it play out in your mind as if you are watching a movie. Use what you wrote down in the previous practice and play the movie in your mind.

This time add feelings to the experience. What will it feel like living your best possible future?

Stand up and align your body language to your best possible future self. Perhaps you are standing up straight with your shoulders back and looking up. Maybe you are pumping your fist in the air, and raising your hands in a victory pose. Act like your best possible future self.

Remember to make this a daily practice until your reality merges with your best possible future.

Regular practice is the key to building this future, to better understand this, think about a tomato seed or any seed of your choice. One day you decide to plant the seeds in your garden. What do you think your expectations of the seed will be? Are you going to expect to get a tomato tree the next day or the next week? No right? You understand the process of growing a tree, and it doesn't happen overnight. You will need to water the seeds daily, make sure it gets enough sunshine, and nurture the soil. It takes around six to eight weeks to grow tomatoes from seed.

The same goes for your ideal future, understand that nature takes time with your ideal future as well. You will need to focus on your ideal future daily. Making sure it plays out in your mind daily and making sure you experience the feeling of the outcome in your body daily. What's more, this process will make your day to day issues more comfortable to get through and increase your happiness and wellbeing.
If your life is challenging right now, you should create an affirmation of your ideal future.

When I was going through a difficult time, I envisioned a better future and visualized it once a day. However, it was not enough because my predominant thoughts were about my issues at the time. Thankfully I recognized this and created an affirmation that reminded me about my ideal future. Every time I thought about my problems, I repeated my affirmations, which made a massive difference in my life.

If you can't come up with an affirmation, use the following one. "My life is now merging with my ideal future" When you say this picture a moment from your ideal future. Doing this is an excellent distraction from your negative thoughts.

Day four
Structured journaling

The previous practice was free-flow journaling, and this practice is structured journaling. Write about any of the following topics:

Before you begin, step into a playful, childlike state, smile, and start writing.

The things I love are

The things that annoy me

My current challenges are

I feel uniquely alive when

When I am at my best I

My favourite way to spend the day is

The things that make me smile are

I cannot imagine my life without this

Day five

Loving Kindness

Put your hand on your heart and say the following phrases out loud.
May I be blessed with loving-kindness

May I feel whole, complete, and calm

May I accept myself just as I am

May all be well in my World

May the joy of being alive nourish my soul.

May I be abundantly happy.

Now say these phrases in your mind.

May I be blessed with loving-kindness

May I feel whole, complete, and calm

May I accept myself just as I am

May all be well in my World

May the joy of being alive nourish my soul.

May I be abundantly happy.

Next bring to mind someone you love, while reading the phrases, keep your hands in the Lotus mudra position, see image below.
Mudras are symbolic hand and finger gestures that assist the flow of energy in the body while enhancing the meditative journey within.

May you be blessed with loving-kindness

May you feel whole, complete, and calm

May you accept yourself just as you are

May you feel the energy of my love now

May the joy of being alive nourish your soul.

May you be abundantly happy.

Now bring to mind somebody you don't know well but see every day, it could be one of your neighbours, a grocery clerk or someone at work. Keep your hands in the lotus mudra position.

May you be blessed with loving-kindness

May you feel whole, complete, and calm

May you accept yourself just as you are

May you feel the energy of my love now

May the joy of being alive nourish your soul.

May you be abundantly happy.
Next, bring to mind someone you don't like. Just for this moment, see if you can let go of feelings of resentment. Keep your hands in the lotus mudra position and say these phrases.

May you be blessed with loving-kindness

May you feel whole, complete, and calm

May you accept yourself just as you are

May you feel the energy of my love now

May the joy of being alive nourish your soul.

May you be abundantly happy.

Next, bring to mind all living beings in the universe. Expand kindness in all directions. Keep your hands in the lotus mudra position and say these phrases.

May all beings be blessed with loving-kindness.

May all beings feel, whole, complete and calm
May all beings accept themselves just as they are

May all beings feel the energy of my love now.

May the joy of being alive nourish every living being.

May all beings be abundantly happy.

Close your eyes, and stay in the energy of kindness for a while. Keep your hands in the lotus mudra position and breathe in through your nose for 4 seconds, breathe out of your nose for 4 seconds and hold your breath for 4 seconds, repeat for a few cycles.

End the session by moving your head side to side, rub your palms together, and finally clench and unclench your fists a few times.

$\mathcal{D}ay$ six

Use your wings

F ind a comfortable place with no distractions. Sit on the floor or on a chair, whichever is more convenient for you.

Step into a childlike, playful state; it is time to
play make-believe. Ready?

You were born with wings but have never used
them, and for this meditation, you are going to use
your wings.
Close your eyes, and bring your wings to the mind.
They are attached to your back.

What colour are they?
How big are they?
How fast do they move?

Feel the power of your wings rush through the rest
of your body.
Feel yourself rise as you begin to fly, you hover in
your current environment. Stay in this moment
for a while and enjoy the feeling.

The rest of this process plays out as you choose. What can you do with these wings? Where can you go? Go there now. Spend the next few minutes going wherever you want to go and do whatever you want to do. When you ready, open your eyes and enjoy the moment.

Now that you know about this energy use it to achieve your goals and come back to this meditation whenever you want to reconnect to this feeling.

Day seven

Alternate nostril breathing

Alternate nostril breathing is an ancient breathing technique that has a therapeutic effect on your health. You can feel the positive effects of it almost immediately.

Begin by blocking your left nostril with your right ring finger, exhale through your right nostril and then inhale through your right nostril. Immediately block your right nostril with your right thumb and exhale through the left nostril and inhale through the left nostril.

Immediately block your left nostril with your right ring finger, exhale through your right nostril and then inhale through your right nostril. Block your right nostril with your right thumb and exhale through the left nostril and inhale through the left nostril.

Continue switching between the two nostrils for 10 minutes.

To have a completely different experience with alternate nostril breathing, try the following.
Block your left nostril with your right ring finger, breathe in and out rapidly for about 3 seconds. Block your right nostril with your right thumb and breathe in and out quickly for about 3 seconds. This type of breathing generates a fantastic feeling.

Books By This Author

Thoughts Of Perfection

*Thoughts of Perfection has helped many people find hope and a will for life. It is an easy read, written in a conversational style designed to uplift you positively.

I found that happiness flows in avalanches of abundance as soon as it comes from within. In this book, you will learn how to attract pleasure and other positive emotions from within. Furthermore, you will learn how to get rid of past burdens and bad memories using a visualization technique. Including a new fantastic way to use affirmations with breath-work.May reading this book help you raise your vibrational energy and help you step into the power of love, peace, and joy.

I wrote this book for those exposed to hardship, emotional pain, crisis, trauma or for those with the following psychological symptoms: Shock, denial, disbelief, confusion, difficulty concentrating, anger, irritability, mood swings, anxiety, fear, guilt, shame, self-blame, withdrawing from

others, feeling sad or hopeless and feeling disconnected or numb.

An Enlightened Path To Self Discovery

Without a life purpose there is no YOU.
Find your life purpose through Self Discovery
In this insightful and highly practical workbook,
Ebrahim Mongratie, an experienced Mindfulness
practitioner and breath-work teacher, condenses
his years of experience in significant bite-sized
chunks of feel-good on-demand techniques. All
derived from modern science and ancient breath-
work principles helping people heal their psyches
and deal with their issues. All these techniques
propel you to self discovery.
You're going to discover a toolbox of 42; time
tested cutting-edge and Powerful feel-good on-demand techniques to help you become the best version of yourself.